Folded Paper
German Stars

0   11557 01456   3

Folded Paper
German Stars

Armin Täubner

STACKPOLE
BOOKS

The original German edition was published as *Das große Fröbelbuch.*
Copyright © 2012 frechverlag GmbH, Stuttgart, Germany (www.frech.de)
This edition is published by arrangement with Claudia Böhme Rights & Literary Agency, Hanover,
Germany (www.agency-boehme.com).

Published by
STACKPOLE BOOKS
5067 Ritter Road
Mechanicsburg, PA 17055
www.stackpolebooks.com

We want to thank Bähr (Kassel), Heyda (Heilbronn) and Rayher (Laupheim) for generously providing
the paper.

PHOTOS: Frechverlag GmbH, 70499 Stuttgart; Michael Ruder Fotografie; Armin Täubner (photos of
work steps and all free-standing images).
ILLUSTRATIONS OF WORK STEPS: Armin Täubner
PRODUCT MANAGEMENT: Claudia Mack
PROOFREADING: Monique Rahner, Schwäbisch Gmünd
LAYOUT: Karoline Steidinger
TRANSLATION: Emily Banwell
COVER DESIGN: Wendy A. Reynolds

Printed in the United States of America

10 9 8 7 6 5 4 3 2 1

First edition

Library of Congress Cataloging-in-Publication Data

Täubner, Armin.
  [Grosse Fröbelbuch. English]
  Folded paper German stars : creative paper crafting ideas inspired by Friedrich Fröbel / by Armin
Täubner.
      pages cm
  Translation of: Das Grosse Fröbelbuch.
  ISBN 978-0-8117-1456-3
  1. Paper work—Germany. 2. Star (Shape) in art. 3. Fröbel, Friedrich, 1782–1852. 4. Activity pro-
grams in education. I. Title.
  TT870.T39313 2015
  745.540943—dc23
                          2014044052

Contents

Symbols Used in This Book

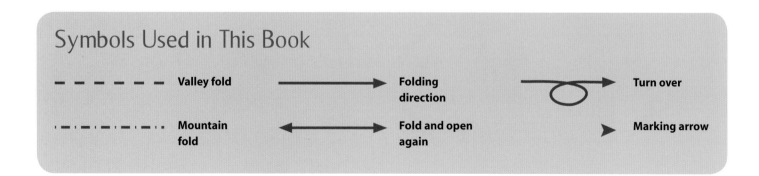

- – – – – – –   **Valley fold**
- ·–·–·–·–·–   **Mountain fold**
- ⟶   **Folding direction**
- ⟷   **Fold and open again**
- ⟲⟶   **Turn over**
- ▶   **Marking arrow**

Preface

Germany's Friedrich Fröbel became world famous for inventing the idea of kindergarten, with games and activities as an important part of childhood education. These activities included paper crafts, which are the subject of this book. Fröbel used these paper crafts, along with other games and activities, to teach children basic mathematical principles and to promote their fine motor, aesthetic, and creative skills.

This book presents a sampling of the folding and weaving techniques that Fröbel developed as teaching tools. These ornate models are designed to be copied directly, but can also serve as a starting point for your own work. Step-by-step instructions are given on folding paper to create basic shapes, which are then the basis of extremely variable ornaments. Another main focus is decorative spheres, built on the same simple shapes. Finally, we introduce weaving with the famous Fröbel star.

All of the projects are explained with easy-to-follow drawings and photos. The individual folding projects are striking by themselves; when they are combined, they become true works of art.

I hope that you, your children, and grandchildren enjoy discovering Fröbel's impressive paper-crafting activities.

Best wishes,

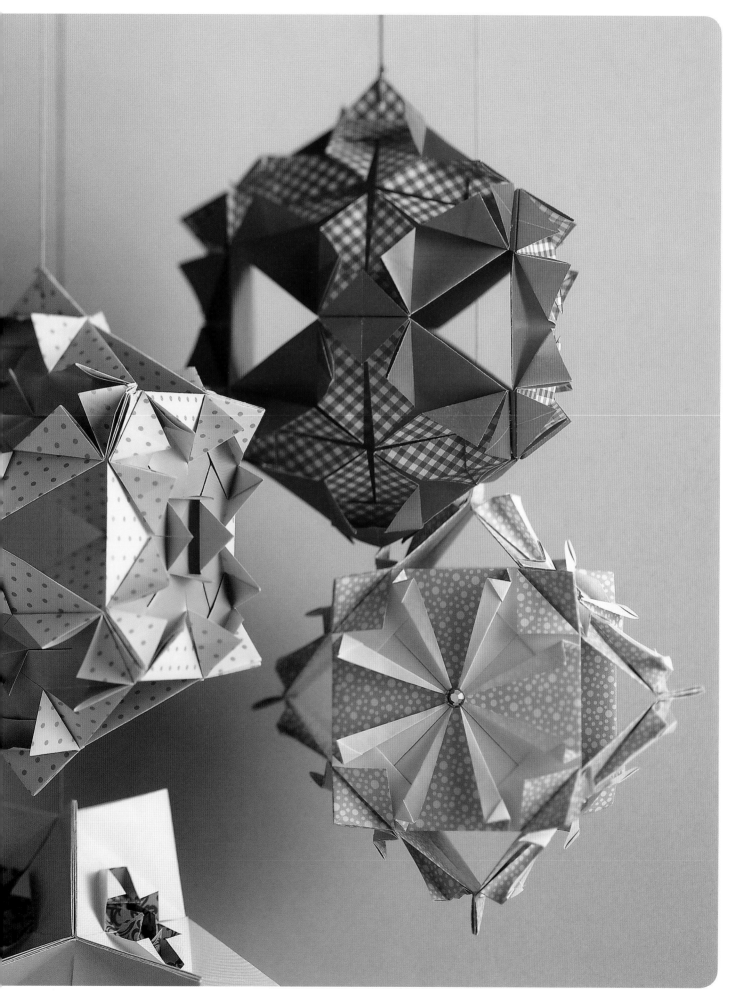

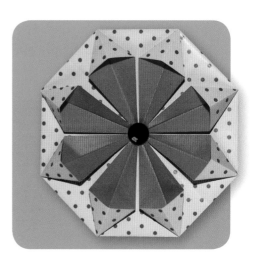

Basic Shapes and Ornaments

Learn the Basic Fröbel Shape with step-by-step instructions, and then use it to create other basic shapes such as medallions and flowers, simply by adding extra folds. These ornaments can then be used for picture frames, candle holders, garlands, and more. Let your imagination run wild!

BASIC FRÖBEL SHAPE

●○○

Finished Size
Approx. 3" x 3" (7.5 x 7.5 cm)

Materials
• 6" x 6" (15 x 15 cm) double-sided origami or other decorative paper

1. Fold the paper diagonally in each direction and open again after each fold.

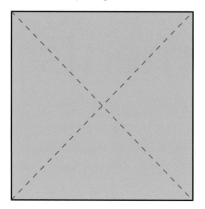

2–3. Fold each of the four corners in toward the center and then back out. Turn the paper over.

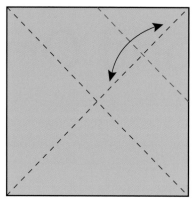

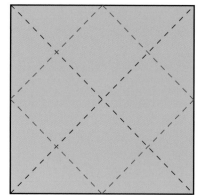

4. This will turn the valley folds into mountain folds.

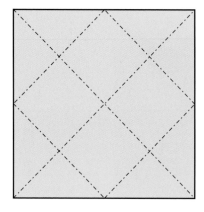

5. Fold the left and right sides toward the center, along the red lines shown here, and then back out.

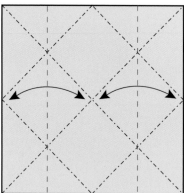

6. Fold the top and bottom toward the center.

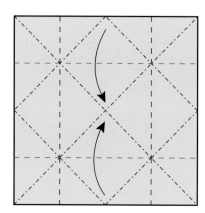

7–8. Now fold the right side in to the left, in the direction of the arrow. This will open up two pockets. Use the existing folded lines to flatten the pockets into squares.

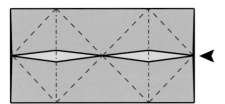 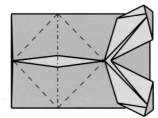

9–10. Repeat on the left side. Now you have the Basic Fröbel Shape.

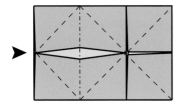 

The Basic Fröbel Shape is the starting point for almost all of the Fröbel patterns, including medallions, crosses, ornaments, and stars.

MEDALLIONS

●●○

Finished Size
Approx. 3" x 3" (7.5 x 7.5 cm)

Materials (for each medallion)
• 6" x 6" (15 x 15 cm) double-sided origami or other decorative paper

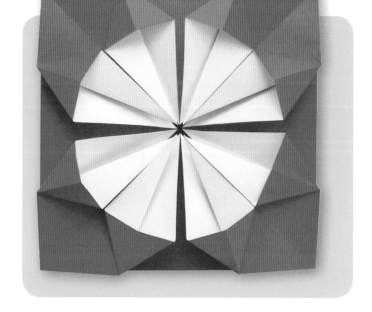

Medallion A

1. Fold the Basic Fröbel Shape as described on pages 12–13. Fold the two sides of the top left square in the direction of the arrows to create a kite shape.

2. Fold the other three squares into a kite shape. Then unfold the sides you have just folded so that they stand upright.

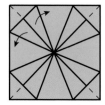

3. Spread open all of the upright wings and flatten them out.

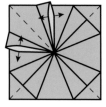 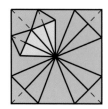 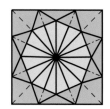

Medallion B

4. Make an ornament as described for Medallion A. Then fold the four corners back along the red lines shown here. This will turn the square medallion into an octagonal medallion.

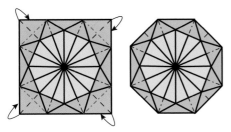

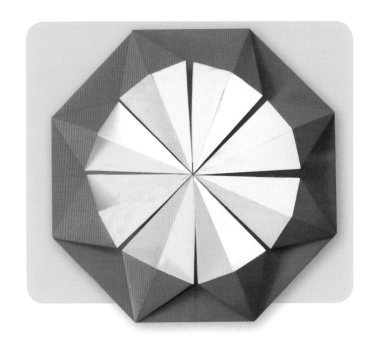

Medallion C

4. Make an ornament as described for Medallion A. Then fold one point from the center of the medallion outward along the red line shown here, in the direction of the arrow.

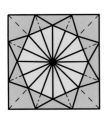 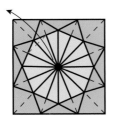 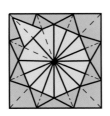

5. Fold the other three points outward in the same way.

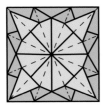

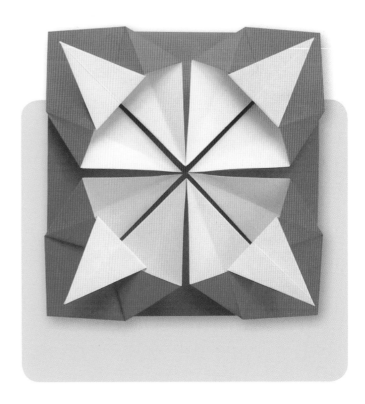

Medallion D

6. This medallion is based on Medallion C. Fold the top point from the center of the medallion upward along the red line shown here, in the direction of the arrow.

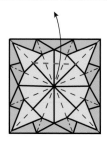

7. Fold the other three points outward from the center in the same way.

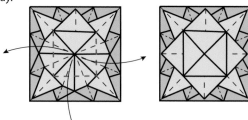

Medallion E

8. This medallion is based on Medallion D. Here, fold the front section of each point that was previously folded outward along the red line shown here, back toward the center of the medallion.

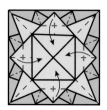 

Foil Ornament

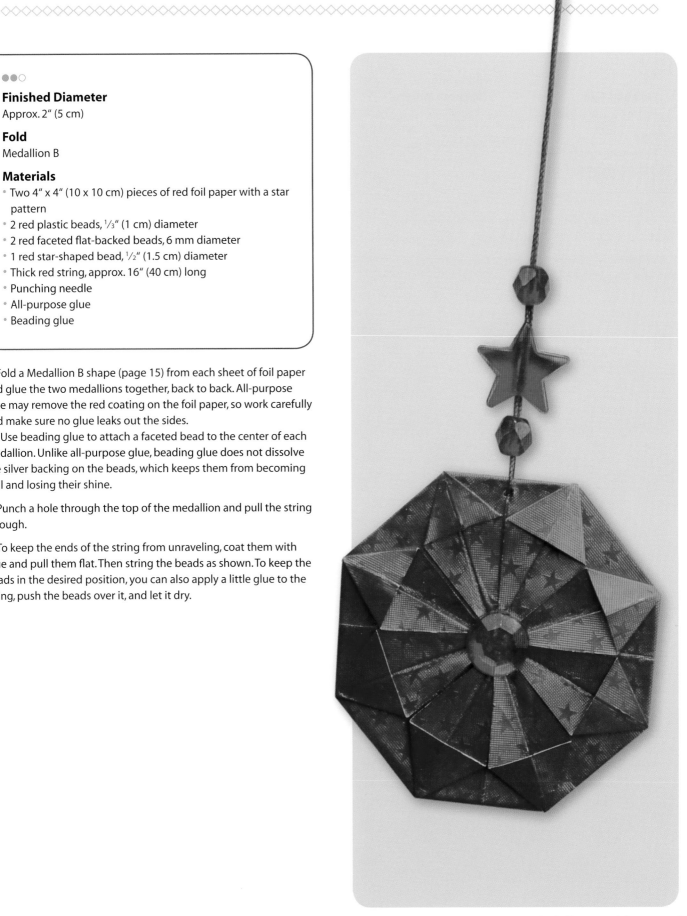

Finished Diameter
Approx. 2" (5 cm)

Fold
Medallion B

Materials
- Two 4" x 4" (10 x 10 cm) pieces of red foil paper with a star pattern
- 2 red plastic beads, $1/3$" (1 cm) diameter
- 2 red faceted flat-backed beads, 6 mm diameter
- 1 red star-shaped bead, $1/2$" (1.5 cm) diameter
- Thick red string, approx. 16" (40 cm) long
- Punching needle
- All-purpose glue
- Beading glue

1. Fold a Medallion B shape (page 15) from each sheet of foil paper and glue the two medallions together, back to back. All-purpose glue may remove the red coating on the foil paper, so work carefully and make sure no glue leaks out the sides.

Use beading glue to attach a faceted bead to the center of each medallion. Unlike all-purpose glue, beading glue does not dissolve the silver backing on the beads, which keeps them from becoming dull and losing their shine.

2. Punch a hole through the top of the medallion and pull the string through.

3. To keep the ends of the string from unraveling, coat them with glue and pull them flat. Then string the beads as shown. To keep the beads in the desired position, you can also apply a little glue to the string, push the beads over it, and let it dry.

Tabletop Lanterns

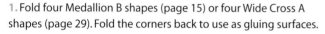

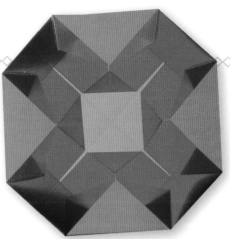

Finished Size
Approx. 4" x 4" (10 x 10 cm)

Fold
Yellow Lantern: Medallion B
Red Lantern: Wide Cross A

Materials
(for each lantern)
• Four 8" x 8" (20 x 20 cm)
  sheets of yellow or red
  translucent paper
• All-purpose glue

1. Fold four Medallion B shapes (page 15) or four Wide Cross A shapes (page 29). Fold the corners back to use as gluing surfaces.

2. Glue the four ornaments together at the corners you have folded back with all-purpose glue.

TIP: For safety reasons, always use a tea light holder or a small hurricane globe inside the lantern.

Picture Frame

●●○

Finished Size
Approx. 3" x 3" (7.5 x 7.5 cm)

Fold
Medallion D

Materials
• 6" x 6" (15 x 15 cm) red/black origami paper with circular pattern
• All-purpose glue
• Photo

1. For the picture frame, fold Medallion D (page 16). You can also fold the corners back to turn the square ornament into an octagon.

2. Cut a photo to 1³⁄₄" x 1³⁄₄" (4.5 x 4.5 cm) and glue it in the center.

TIP: You can glue several of these picture frames together, as shown for the wall hanging on page 38, to create a small gallery.

Medallion Garlands

Finished Size
Approx. 3" x 3" (7.5 x 7.5 cm), each ornament

Fold
Red Garland: Medallions A and B (pages 14 and 15)
Turquoise Garland: Wide Cross A (page 29) and Open Cross Flower C (page 33)

Materials
- 6" x 6" (15 x 15 cm) red/pink or turquoise/light blue origami paper with a polka-dot pattern
- Red or turquoise crochet thread
- Your choice of beads
- Punching needle
- All-purpose glue

1. These garlands can be made with any of the ornaments in this book. The ornaments are threaded onto the garland by punching a hole on each side with the punching needle.

2. Coat the end of the thread with a little bit of glue and twist it so that it is stiff and can easily be threaded through the ornaments. You can string beads in between the ornaments, if you wish.

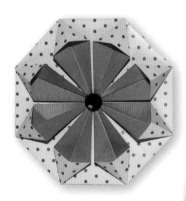

STARS

●●○

Finished Size
Approx. 3" (7.5 cm)

Fold
Basic Fröbel Shape

Materials (for each star)
• 6" x 6" (15 x 15 cm) double-sided origami paper

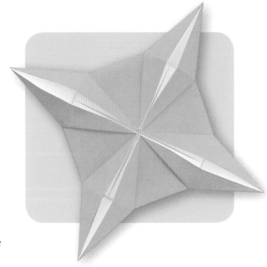

Star A

1. Fold the Basic Fröbel Shape (page 12), and then fold the two sides of the top left square inward in the direction of the arrows to create a kite shape.

2. Repeat with the other three squares. Then fold the corner of the top left square backward at the red line shown here, and forward again.

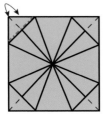

3. Unfold the sides of the top left-hand kite shape again.

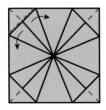

4. Fold the point outward from the center, following the red line shown here.

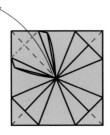 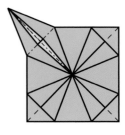

5. Repeat with the other three points.

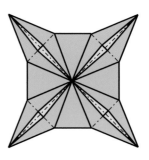

Star B

6. Fold Star B in the same way as Star A, and then turn it over.

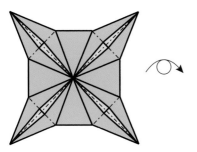 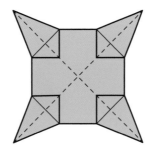

Star C

6. Fold Star C in the same way as Star A.

7. The four slightly opened star points will close when you fold the four corners outward from the center, along the red line shown here.

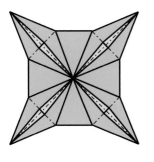 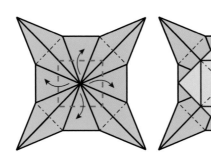

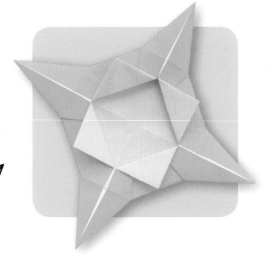

Star D

8. Fold this star the same way as Star C. Then fold the points of the corners back inward, following the red line shown here.

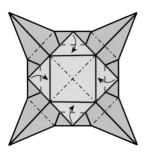 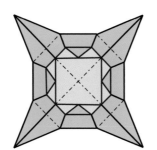

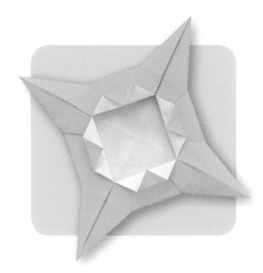

Double Star

Finished Size
Approx. 8" (20 cm)

Fold
Star A

Materials
- Two 8" x 8" (20 x 20 cm) double-sided sheets of patterned origami paper
- All-purpose glue, if needed

1. Fold two Star A shapes (page 22) for each double star.

2. Place the two four-pointed stars back to back with the points offset.

3. Next, fold the four short interior points over the straight edges between the long points of the other star. This allows you to combine the two four-pointed stars into an eight-pointed star without using any glue. (You can always apply a little glue to be on the safe side.)

Candle Coaster

Finished Size
Approx. 6" (15 cm)

Fold
Stars A and D

Materials (for each star)
• Two 6" x 6" (15 x 15 cm) double-sided sheets of patterned origami paper
• All-purpose glue

1. Fold one Star A shape (page 22) and one Star D shape (page 23) for each candle coaster.

2. Glue Star D to Star A, offsetting them to create an eight-pointed star. The unfolded center area can be adjusted slightly to the size of the tea light by moving the red fold line (shown in the instructions for Star D on page 23) slightly outward.

CROSSES

Narrow Cross

●●○

Finished Size
Approx. 3" x 3" (7.5 x 7.5 cm)

Fold
The Basic Fröbel Shape is the starting point. The six

variations use many of the same folds.

**Materials
(for each cross)**
• 6" x 6" (15 x 15 cm) double-sided origami paper

Narrow Cross A

1. Fold the Basic Fröbel Shape (page 12). Fold the sides of the top left square inward, in the direction of the arrows and along the red line shown here, to create a kite shape.

2. Repeat with the other three squares.

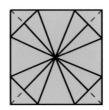

Narrow Cross B

1. Fold the Basic Fröbel Shape (page 12). Fold the corner of the top left square outward, in the direction of the arrow along the red line.

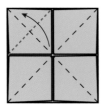

2. Repeat with the other three squares, folding the corners outward.

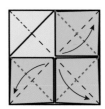
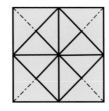

3. Now fold the sides of the top left square inward, in the direction of the arrows and along the red line shown here, to create a kite shape.

 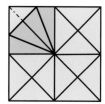

4. Repeat with the other three squares.

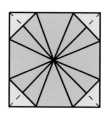

Narrow Cross C

5. This model is a continuation of Narrow Cross B. Starting with the top left kite shape, fold the two corners in the direction of the arrows, along the red lines shown here.

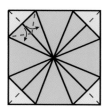 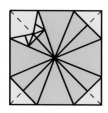

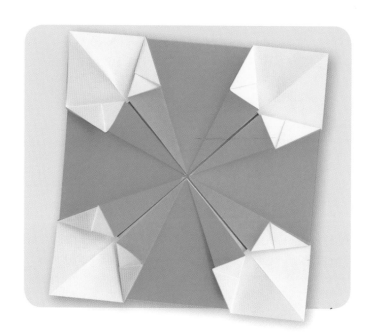

6. Repeat with the other three kite shapes.

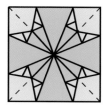

Narrow Cross D

7. This cross is a continuation of Narrow Cross C. Fold the four corners inward along the red lines shown here.

 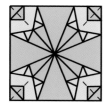

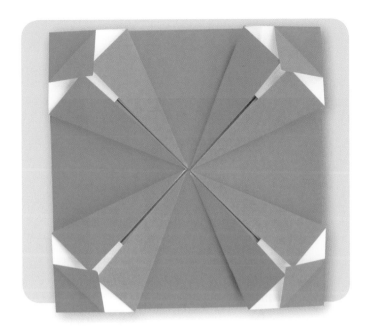

Narrow Cross E

5. This cross is a continuation of Narrow Cross A. Fold the four corners inward along the red lines shown here.

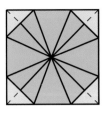 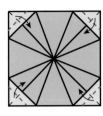 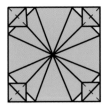

6. Slide the points of the inward-folded corners under the kite shapes.

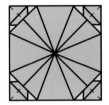

Narrow Cross F

3. This cross is a continuation of Narrow Cross B, up to step 2. Fold the corners of the four squares in the direction of the arrows, along the red lines shown here.

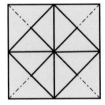 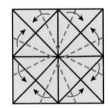 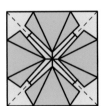

Wide Cross

●○○

Finished Size
Approx. 3" x 3" (7.5 x 7.5 cm)

Fold
The Basic Fröbel Shape is the starting point. The six variations use many of the same folds.

Materials (for each cross)
• 6" x 6" (15 x 15 cm) double-sided origami paper

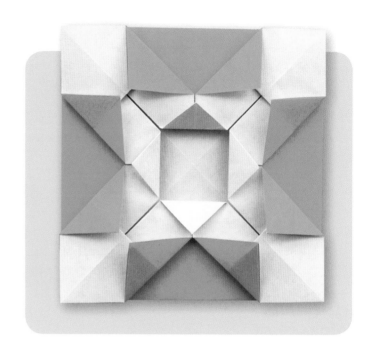

Wide Cross A

1. Fold the Basic Fröbel Shape (page 12). Then fold the corner of the top left square outward, in the direction of the arrow and along the red line shown here.

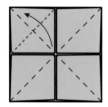

2. Repeat with the corners of the other three squares.

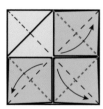 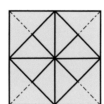

3. Fold two corners of a square inward along the red lines shown here.

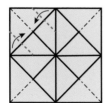

4. Repeat with the other three squares, folding inward along the red lines.

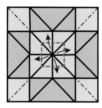 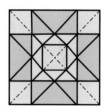

5. Fold the four points outward from the center, along the red lines shown here.

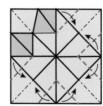 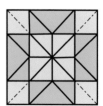

Wide Cross B

3. Steps 1–2 are identical to Wide Cross A. Next, fold two corners of a square inward along the red lines shown here.

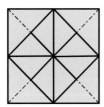 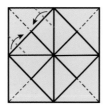

4. Repeat with the other three squares, folding inward along the red lines.

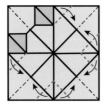 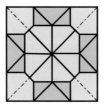

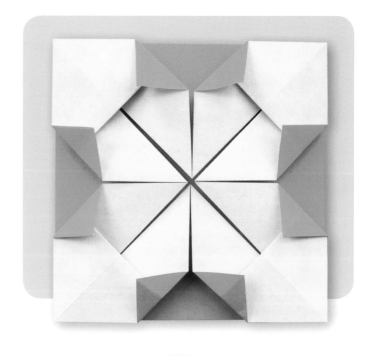

Wide Cross C

3. Steps 1–2 are identical to Wide Cross A. Next, fold the four corners in the direction of the arrows, following the red lines shown here.

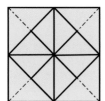 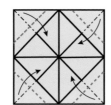 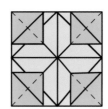

Wide Cross D

4. Steps 1–3 are identical to Wide Cross C. Next, fold the corners outward along the red lines shown here.

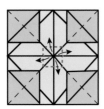 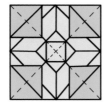

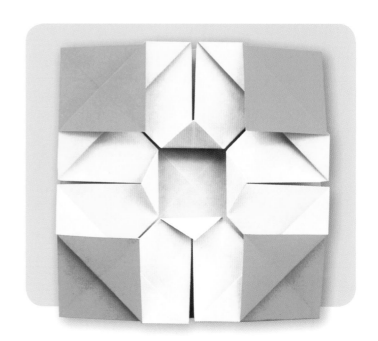

Wide Cross E

1. Start with the Basic Fröbel Shape (page 12) and fold the four inner corners outward in the direction of the arrows, along the red lines shown here.

 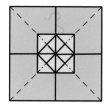

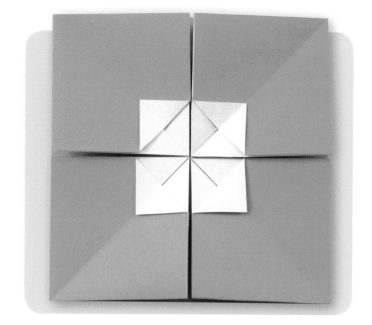

Wide Cross F

1. Start with the Basic Fröbel Shape (page 12) and fold the four inner corners outward in the direction of the arrows, along the red lines shown here.

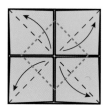 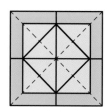

2. Then fold the four inner corners outward in the direction of the arrows, along the red lines shown here.

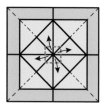 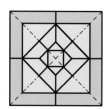

Open Cross Flower

●●○

Finished Size
Approx. 3" x 3" (7.5 x 7.5 cm)

Fold
The Basic Fröbel Shape is the starting point. The six variations use many of the same folds.

Materials (for each Open Cross Flower)
• 6" x 6" (15 x 15 cm) double-sided origami paper

Open Cross Flower A

1. Start with the Basic Fröbel Shape (page 12) and fold two corners of a square inward, in the direction of the arrows and along the red lines shown here, to create a kite shape.

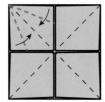

2. Repeat with the other three squares.

 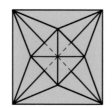

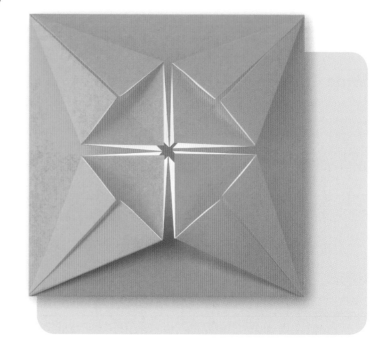

Open Cross Flower B

3. This model is based on Open Cross Flower A, but four triangles are folded outward from the center along the red lines shown here.

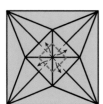 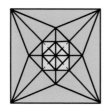

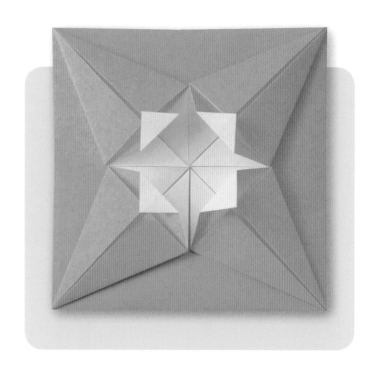

Open Cross Flower C

3. This model is based on Open Cross Flower A. Next, fold the four triangles outward from the center in the direction of the arrows, along the red lines. Open Cross Flower C is similar to model B, but the triangles are larger.

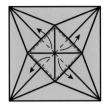 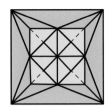

Open Cross Flower D

4. This cross flower is based on Open Cross Flower C. Fold the points of the triangles back inward.

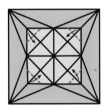 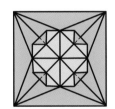

Open Cross Flower E

5. This Cross Flower is based on Open Cross Flower D. Next, fold the points outward from the center, along the red lines shown here.

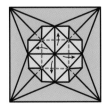 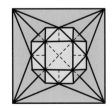

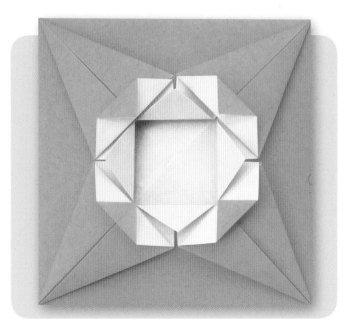

Open Cross Flower F

1. Fold the Basic Fröbel Shape (page 12). Then fold the inner edge of each square outward in the direction of the arrows, along the red lines shown here.

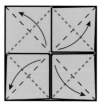 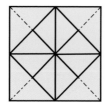

2. Fold two corners of each square in the direction of the arrows, along the red lines.

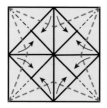

3. Now fold the eight corners in the direction of the arrows, along the red lines.

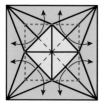 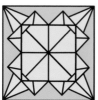

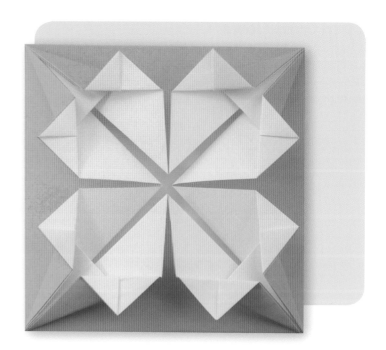

Open Cross Flower G

1. Fold the Basic Fröbel Shape (page 12). Then fold the inner corners of the four squares outward along the red lines shown here.

2. Next, fold two corners of each square in the direction of the arrows, along the red lines.

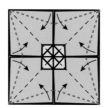 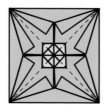

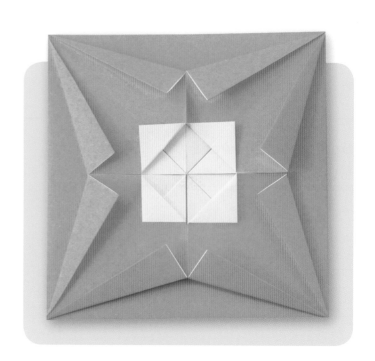

Covered Cross Flower

●●○

Finished Size
Approx. 3" x 3" (7.5 x 7.5 cm)

Fold
The Basic Fröbel Shape is the starting point. The three variations of the Covered

Cross Flower use many of the same folds.

Materials (for each cross flower)
• 6" x 6" (15 x 15 cm) double-sided origami paper

Covered Cross Flower A

1. Fold the Basic Fröbel Shape (page 12). Fold the right side of one square down over the left side, along the red line.

2. Next, fold the left side of the triangle that you just folded back to the right, along the red line.

5. Repeat with the other three squares.

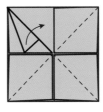 

3. Fold this triangle to the right.

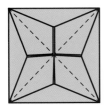   

4. Repeat with the left side of the same square.

6. Next, fold the four inner corners outward along the red lines.

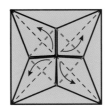 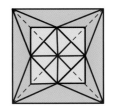

Covered Cross Flower B

7. This flower is based on Covered Cross Flower A. The next step is to fold the inner corners outward one more time.

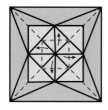

8. Next, fold the indicated points inward again.

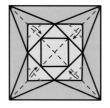 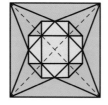

Covered Cross Flower C

1. Fold the Basic Fröbel Shape (page 12). Fold the inner half of each square outward along the red line.

 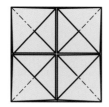

2. Fold the right half of the top left square to the left, along the red line.

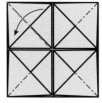 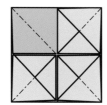

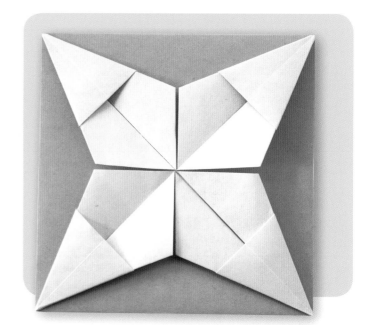

3. Take the half you just folded over and fold it back to the right, along the red line.

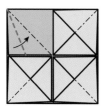

4. Fold the resulting triangle back to the right, along the red line.

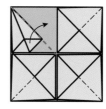 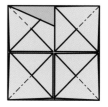

5. Repeat with the left half of the same square by folding the left side to the right along the red line.

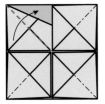 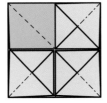

7. Fold the resulting triangle back to the left, along the red line.

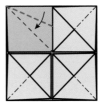

6. Take the half you just folded over and fold it back to the left, along the red line.

 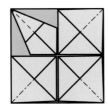

8. Repeat steps 2–7 with the other three squares.

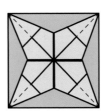

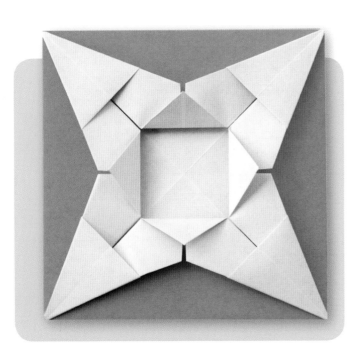

Covered Cross Flower D

9. This model is based on Covered Cross Flower C. Next, fold one point from the center along the red line shown here.

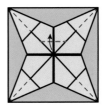 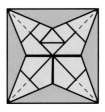

10. Repeat with the other three points.

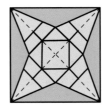

Wall Hanging

◇◇◇◇◇◇◇◇◇◇◇◇◇◇◇◇◇◇◇◇◇◇

●●●

Finished Size (each ornament)
Approx. 3" x 3" (7.5 x 7.5 cm)

Fold
Varies by ornament

Materials
- Sixteen 6" x 6" (15 x 15 cm) pieces of double-sided origami or craft paper (yellow/blue paper is used here)
- 12" x 12" (30 x 30 cm) thick cardboard or paperboard
- All-purpose glue

1. Cut the pieces of paper to size from origami paper or a roll of double-sided craft paper.

2. You can vary the size of the finished wall hanging by adding as many ornaments as you like. The only important thing is for half of the ornaments to have the blue (dark) side facing up and the other half the yellow (light) side up to create the varied color effects.

3. There are hundreds of possible variations—a few of them are shown here. You can fold many of the ornaments by following the folding diagrams on the previous pages. For some ornaments, corners have also been folded outward or inward.

4. Arrange the finished ornaments on the cardboard to create a balanced pattern. Then glue the ornaments down, one at a time.

Wide Cross C variation	Open Cross Flower G variation	Narrow Cross E	Covered Cross Flower C variation
Wide Cross F	Wide Cross C	Open Cross Flower B	Narrow Cross B
Narrow Cross B variation (covered)*	Wide Cross A variation	Narrow Cross D	Wide Cross A variation
Wide Cross D	Covered Cross Flower C	Open Cross Flower G variation	Open Cross Flower G variation

* This variation is folded as follows: in steps 1–2, do not fold the corners all the way to the center. In steps 3–4, fold the sides back instead of upward.

Wall Hanging in Candy Colors

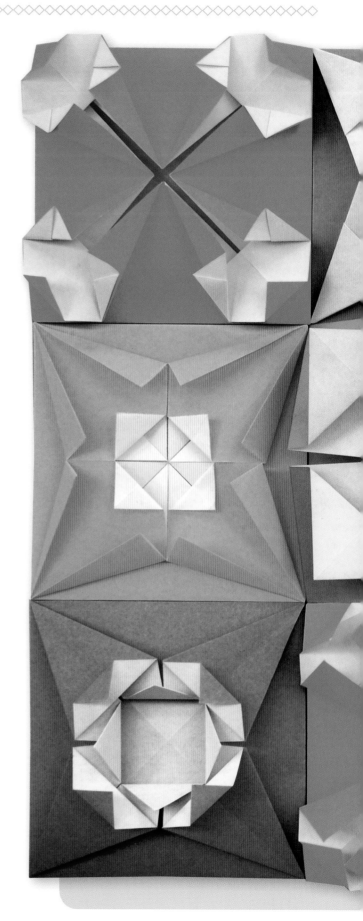

○●○

Finished Size (each ornament)
Approx. 3" x 3" (7.5 x 7.5 cm)

Fold
Varies by ornament

Materials
- Three 6" x 6" (15 x 15 cm) sheets each of pink, light green, purple, and blue origami paper
- 12" x 12" (30 x 30 cm) thick cardboard or paperboard
- All-purpose glue

1. You can vary the size of the finished wall handing by adding as many ornaments as you like. You can also use any ornaments you like in the piece.

2. The ornaments shown here can be found in the chart below. Fold the ornaments by following the instructions on the previous pages.

3. Arrange the finished ornaments on the cardboard to create a balanced pattern. Then glue the ornaments down, one at a time.

Narrow Cross D	Covered Cross D	Open Cross Flower B	Wide Cross A
Open Cross Flower G	Wide Cross F	Narrow Cross F	Open Cross Flower F
Covered Cross Flower B	Narrow Cross E	Wide Cross E	Covered Cross Flower C

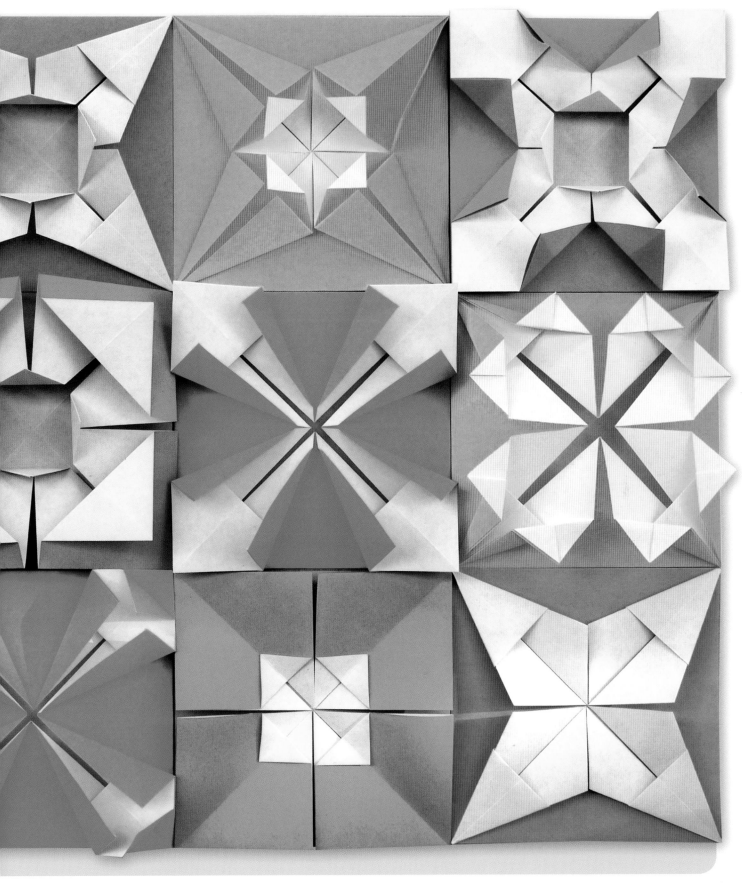

Star Garland

Finished Size (each ornament)
Approx. 3" x 3" (7.5 x 7.5 cm)

Fold
Open Cross Flower F and Narrow Cross F

Materials
- 6" x 6" (15 x 15 cm) green/white origami paper with snowflakes and stars
- Light green crochet thread
- Light green single-sided beads, 6 mm diameter (4 per ornament)
- Dark green single-sided beads, 8 mm diameter (1 or 4 per ornament, as shown)
- Round beads, 8 mm diameter
- Punching needle
- All-purpose glue

1. Any ornaments can be used for these garlands. In this example, we combined the Open Cross Flower F (page 34) and Narrow Cross F (page 28) models. Fold the ornaments according to the instructions. Glue single-sided beads on the ornaments, as shown.

2. Use the needle to punch a hole on either side of each ornament.

3. Coat the end of the crochet thread with a little bit of glue and twist it so that it stays stiff and is easier to pull through the holes in the ornaments.

4. String ornaments and beads on crochet thread, as shown.

Transparent Window Stars

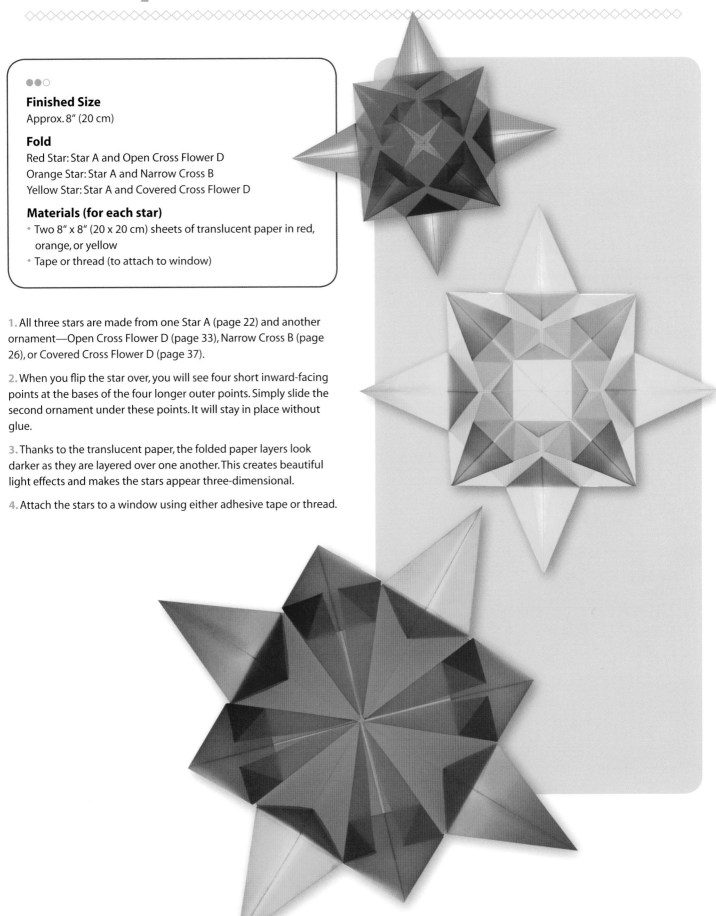

●●○

Finished Size
Approx. 8″ (20 cm)

Fold
Red Star: Star A and Open Cross Flower D
Orange Star: Star A and Narrow Cross B
Yellow Star: Star A and Covered Cross Flower D

Materials (for each star)
• Two 8″ x 8″ (20 x 20 cm) sheets of translucent paper in red, orange, or yellow
• Tape or thread (to attach to window)

1. All three stars are made from one Star A (page 22) and another ornament—Open Cross Flower D (page 33), Narrow Cross B (page 26), or Covered Cross Flower D (page 37).

2. When you flip the star over, you will see four short inward-facing points at the bases of the four longer outer points. Simply slide the second ornament under these points. It will stay in place without glue.

3. Thanks to the translucent paper, the folded paper layers look darker as they are layered over one another. This creates beautiful light effects and makes the stars appear three-dimensional.

4. Attach the stars to a window using either adhesive tape or thread.

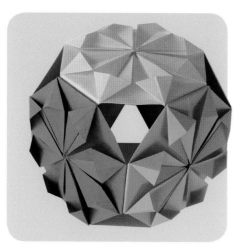

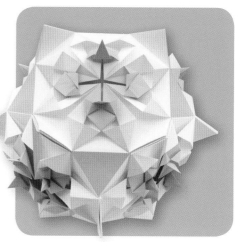

Spheres

The basic modules for the spheres are the ornaments you learned in the chapter on Basic Shapes and Ornaments, for which there are many hundreds of variations. You can make countless different spheres using either six or twelve ornaments. The options increase further depending on the paper you choose.

SIMPLE CUBED SPHERE

●●○

Finished Diameter
Approx. 3¹/₂" (9 cm)

Fold
Start with the Basic Fröbel Shape. The gluing corners are on the outside.

Materials
• Six 6" x 6" (15 x 15 cm) sheets of lilac-colored origami paper with purple/pink pattern
• All-purpose glue

1. Fold the Basic Fröbel Shape (page 12), then fold the four corners in toward the center and then back out, along the red lines shown here.

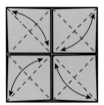

4. Turn the ornaments over, coat the corners with glue (yellow lines), and glue them together into a cube.

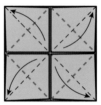

2. Next, fold the upper layer outward from the center. Now the ornament has changed color from purple to pink.

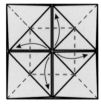 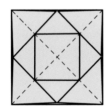 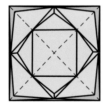

3. Fold the inner corners outward along the red lines so that a square pink surface is created in the center. The unfolded triangles will stand up at a slight angle. Fold five more ornaments in the same way.

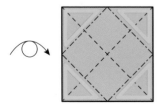

● ● ○

Finished Diameter

Approx. 3¹/₂" (9 cm)

Fold

Start with the Basic Fröbel Shape. The gluing corners are on the outside.

Materials

• Six 6" x 6" (15 x 15 cm) sheets of lilac-colored origami paper with purple/pink pattern
• All-purpose glue

1. Fold the Basic Fröbel Shape (page 12), then fold the four corners toward the center along the red lines, and back outward again.

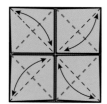

2. Fold the inner corners outward along the red lines to create a small square purple area in the center.

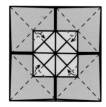

3. Fold the points of the unfolded triangles back toward the center, along the red lines.

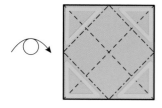

4. Fold the inner corners outward along the red lines. This will reveal the purple patterned surface underneath. Fold five more ornaments.

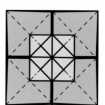

5. Turn the ornaments over, coat the corners with glue (yellow lines), and glue them together into a cube.

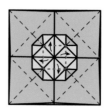
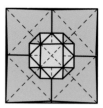

WIDE CROSS SPHERE

● ● ○

Finished Diameter
Approx. 5½" (14 cm)

Fold
Wide Cross A ornament.
The gluing corners for this
sphere are on the outside.

Materials
- Six 6" x 6" (15 x 15 cm)
  sheets of origami paper,
  yellow and light green
  with polka dots or red and
  white with checks
- All-purpose glue

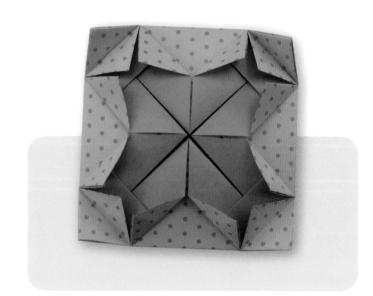

1. Follow steps 1–4 for Wide Cross A (page 29) to fold six ornaments. In the variation shown here the center of the ornament has not been folded open (skip step 5 for Wide Cross A). Fold the four gluing edges forward and then back again to the outside.

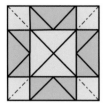 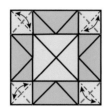

2. Fold the top layer of paper back toward the center at each corner, along the red lines. Turn the ornament over. The yellow lines on the corners represent the gluing edges.

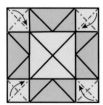 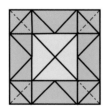 

3. Arrange the ornaments next to each other as shown in the photo, and glue the edges together.

4. Turn the project over.

5. Fold two ornaments upward and glue them together.

6. Next, fold another ornament upward and glue it on to create the third side wall.

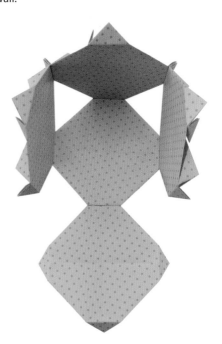

7. Glue on the fourth side wall. Now all that is missing is the lid. Glue that on as well.

8. Now the sphere is finished.

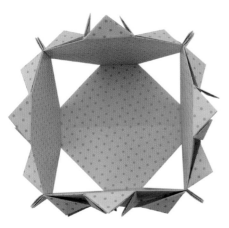

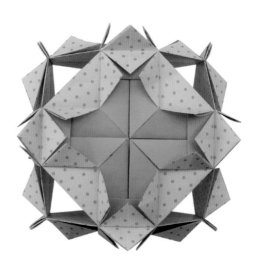

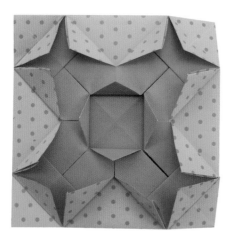

The steps for the red-and-white sphere are the same as for the yellow-and-green sphere (without the unfolded centers). Here, the glued edges are on the inside, pointing toward the center of the sphere.

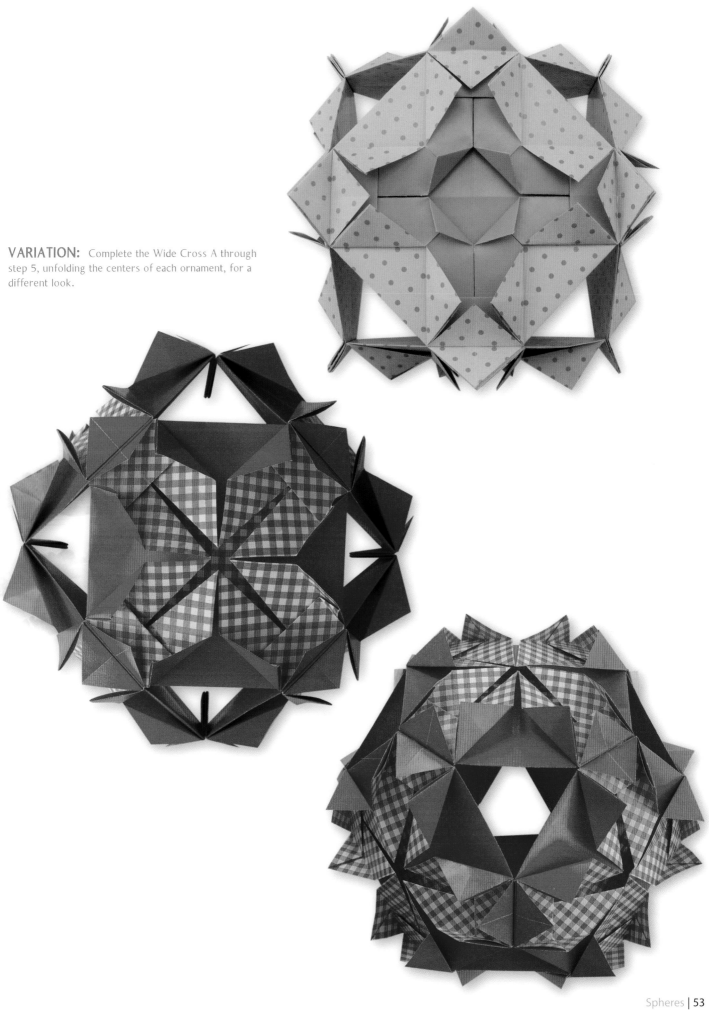

VARIATION: Complete the Wide Cross A through step 5, unfolding the centers of each ornament, for a different look.

NARROW CROSS SPHERE

●●○

Finished Diameter
Approx. 5½" (14 cm)

Fold
Narrow Cross B ornament. The gluing corners are on the outside.

Materials
• Six 6" x 6" (15 x 15 cm) sheets of light blue origami paper with white dots
• 6 light blue plastic sequins, 5 mm diameter
• All-purpose glue
• Beading glue

1. Make the Narrow Cross B ornament (page 26) and continue folding. Fold the edges back outward along the red lines shown here.

2. Fold the top layer of each of the four corners inward along the red lines.

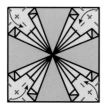 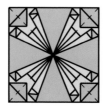

3. Fold the four remaining corners inward too, and then unfold them again. Fold five more ornaments, and then glue on the sequins, using beading glue. Unlike all-purpose glue, this type of glue does not dissolve the silver backing on the sequins and keeps them from turning dull.

4. Turn the ornaments over, apply glue to the yellow corners shown here, and glue the sphere together, as shown on page 55.

 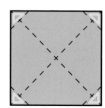

STAR SPHERE

Finished Diameter
Approx. 7" (18 cm)

Fold
Stars A and B ornaments. The gluing corners are on the inside.

Materials
• Six 6" x 6" (15 x 15 cm) sheets of red origami paper with a gold floral pattern
• All-purpose glue

1. Use the sheets to fold six Star A ornaments (page 22).

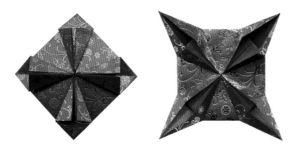

2. Turn the ornament over to create Star B (page 23). The marked yellow areas in the illustration are the gluing surfaces.

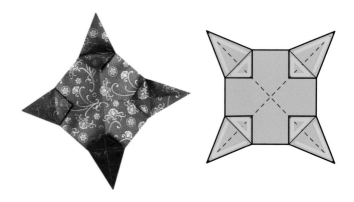

3. Apply glue to the gluing edges and the points of two of these inverted ornaments. The two edges you have glued together will point up, while the longer glued-together points will point down and are not visible in this picture.

4. Glue on another ornament in the same way. This third ornament is initially glued only to one of the other two ornaments.

5. Now also glue it to the other ornament.

6. Glue on the fourth ornament.

7. Now glue on the fifth ornament.

8. The last ornament has now been glued on, and the sphere is finished. Now spread open the folds along the points. They will have closed up when you glued the ornaments together, but they are easy to unfold again.

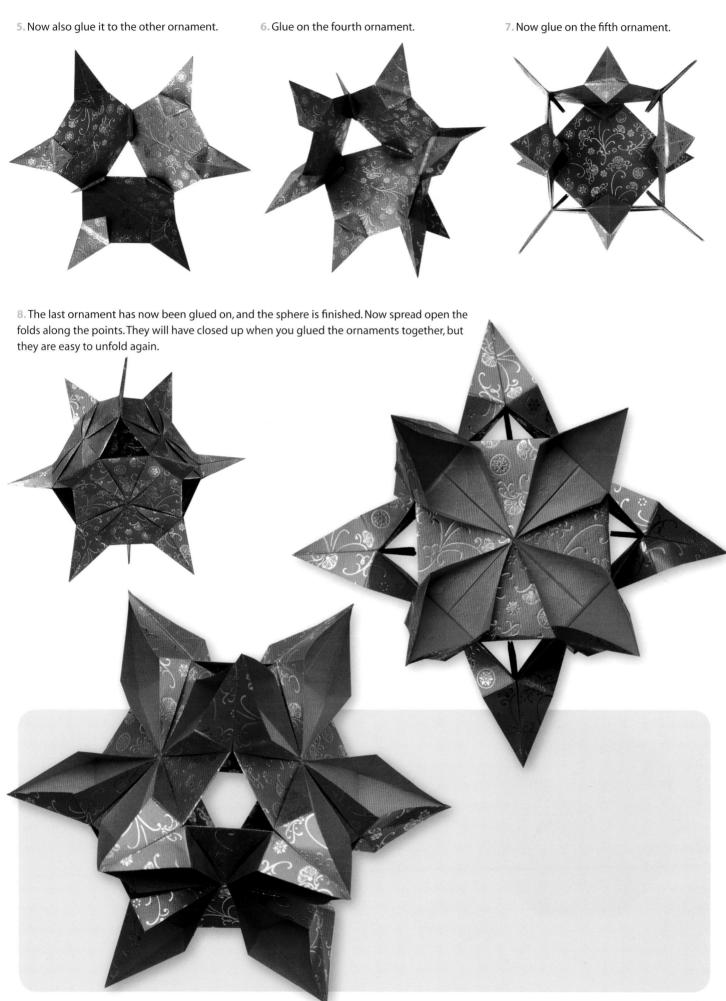

ROSE SPHERE

●●●

Finished Diameter
Approx. 7" (18 cm)

Fold
Narrow Cross A ornament. The gluing
corners are on the inside.

Materials
- Six 8" x 8" (20 x 20 cm) sheets of lilac
  origami paper with vine pattern
- Six 4" x 4" (10 x 10 cm) sheets of lilac
  origami paper with vine pattern All-
  purpose glue

1. Make the Narrow Cross A (page 26), and fold the four corners backward along the red lines shown here.

2. The corners that have been folded back are the gluing edges. Now unfold the kite shapes.

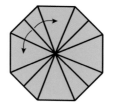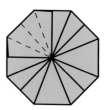

3. Next, roll the four corners outward from the center.

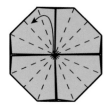

4. Fold the inner corner outward and then back again, along the red line. Repeat with the other three corners.

5. Finally, fold the points of the corners outward again, along the red lines. Make five more ornaments.

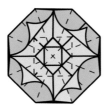

Assembly: Follow the folding steps for the six small and six large sheets, but for the smaller sheets, skip step 5. Glue a small ornament inside each of the larger ornaments. Apply glue to the four folded-back gluing edges of each large ornament and glue the ornaments together to make a sphere. You can follow the gluing instructions on pages 60–61, but with the gluing edges facing inward.

SIMPLE MEDALLION SPHERE

○●○

Finished Diameter
Approx. 2¼" (6 cm)

Fold
Medallion A ornament

Materials
- Two 4" x 4" (10 x 10 cm) sheets each of origami paper in light pink, dark pink, and hot pink or yellow, light green, and dark green
- All-purpose glue

Note: The spheres are different colors, but the pink sphere also has the gluing edges folded forward, which means they will be visible later on as outside points. In the green version, they are folded backward, so they are hidden.

1. Fold two Medallion A ornaments (page 14) in each color. Fold the gluing edges forward for the pink sphere. The illustrations on the left below show the folds and gluing surfaces for the pink sphere, and the illustrations on the right show the same for the green sphere.

 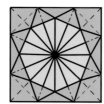 

Gluing surfaces, outside (pink sphere)

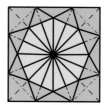 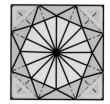

Gluing surfaces, inside (green sphere)

2. Arrange the medallions as shown in the picture below, and glue them together along the gluing edges. Here, for the pink sphere, the gluing edges point up; that means they will point outward when the sphere is finished. For the green sphere, the gluing edges point down, so they will be on the inside of the finished sphere.

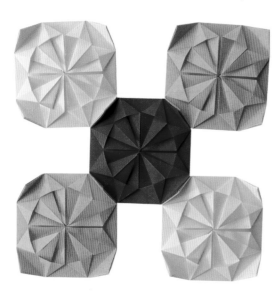

3. Fold two medallions upward to act as the side walls, and glue them together along the gluing edges.

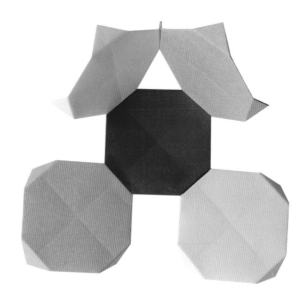

4. Fold another ornament upward and glue the edges together.

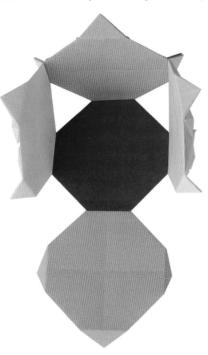

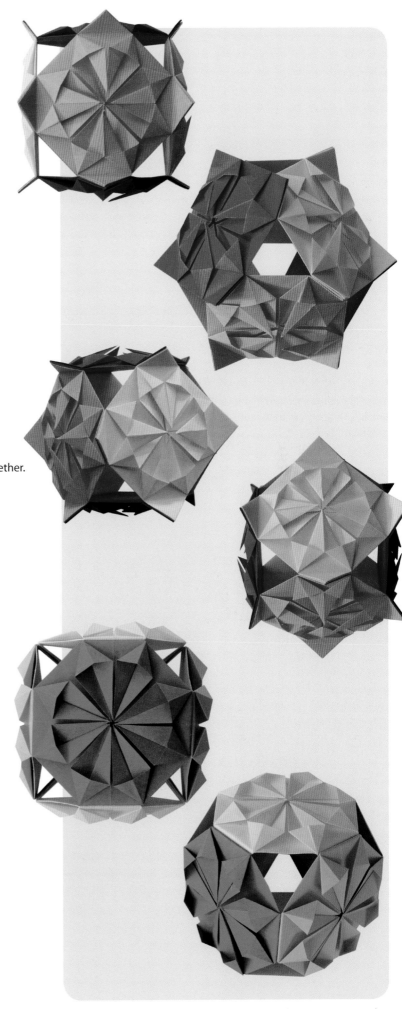

5. Four side walls have now been folded upward and glued together.

6. Glue the sixth ornament on as a lid.

SQUARE MEDALLION SPHERE WITH FLOWER

● ● ●

Finished Diameter
Approx. 7" (18 cm)

Fold
White Origami Sheets: Medallion A ornament

Light Blue Origami Sheets: Medallion C ornament
For this sphere, the gluing edges are on the outside.

Materials
- Six 8" x 8" (20 x 20 cm) sheets of white origami paper
- Six 4" x 4" (10 x 10 cm) sheets of light blue origami paper
- All-purpose glue

1. Use the white sheets to fold six Medallion A ornaments (see page 14) with the gluing edges on the outside (folded forward, as in the illustration). Use the light blue sheets to fold six Medallion C ornaments (page 15).

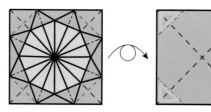

Gluing edges on the outside (white medallion)

2. Place the light blue ornament on top of the white ornament. Lift one of the white inner points and slide the small ornament underneath it.

3. Slide the small ornament under the other three inner points. Make five more double ornaments.

4. Glue five of the double ornaments together along the gluing edges.

5. Fold two of the double ornaments down and glue them together to create two side walls.

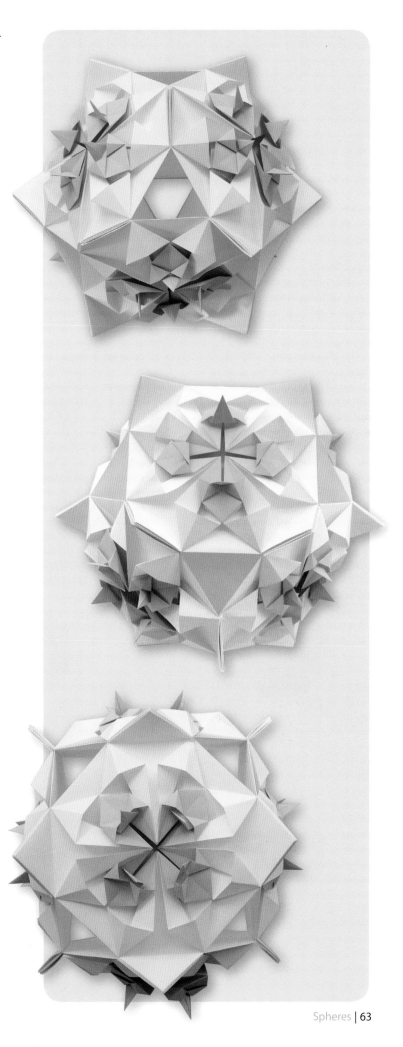

6. Fold the other two double ornaments down and glue them together as well. Now five sides of the cube are finished.

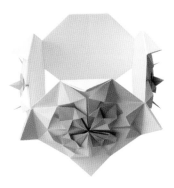

7. Glue on the sixth side to finish the medallion sphere.

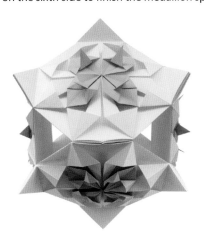

OCTAGONAL MEDALLION SPHERE WITH FLOWER

●●●

Finished Diameter
Approx. 5½" (14 cm)

Fold
Purple Origami Sheets: Medallion B ornament
Lilac Origami Sheets: Narrow Cross D ornament

Materials
• Six 8" x 8" (20 x 20 cm) sheets of purple origami paper
• Six 4" x 4" (10 x 10 cm) sheets of lilac origami paper
• All-purpose glue

1. Use the purple sheets to fold six Medallion B ornaments (page 15). This medallion will have four gluing edges on the back.

 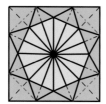 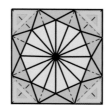

2. Fold the lilac sheets to create six Narrow Cross D ornaments (page 27).

3. Place the lilac ornament on top of the purple ornament. Lift one of the inner corners and slide the small ornament underneath it.

4. Slide the small ornament under the other three inner points. Make five more double ornaments.

5. Turn the double ornaments over.

6. Next, glue two double ornaments together along the gluing edges.

7. Here, five double ornaments have been glued together.

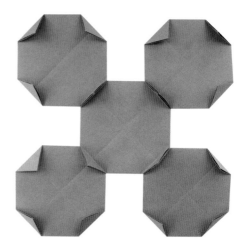

8. Fold two of the double ornaments upward and glue them together to create two side walls.

9. Fold another double ornament upward and glue it on.

10. Now four double ornaments have been folded upward and glued together.

11. Glue the last double ornament on as the lid.

You can use these elegant medallion spheres as decorations in your home or in a window. Simply punch a hole with a needle and thread them onto a matching piece of string to hang them up.

Fröbel Stars

Fröbel Stars, known by a variety of names, are commonly used as Christmas decorations. Traditionally, they were dipped in wax and sprinkled with glitter, which you could certainly try on any of the projects in this book for added sparkle. To begin any of these three-dimensional stars, you'll need four paper strips with a width-to-length ratio of 1:30.

FRÖBEL STAR

●●●

Finished Size

Approx. 1½" (4 cm)

Materials

• 4 paper strips of the same size, with a width-to-length ratio of 1:30, such as ⅓" x 12" (1 x 30 cm)

1–4. Fold each of the paper strips in half and weave them together to create a cross shape.

1

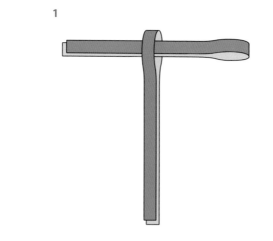

2

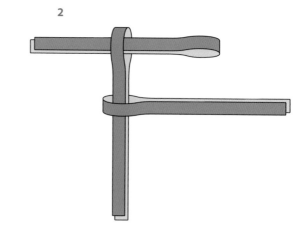

3

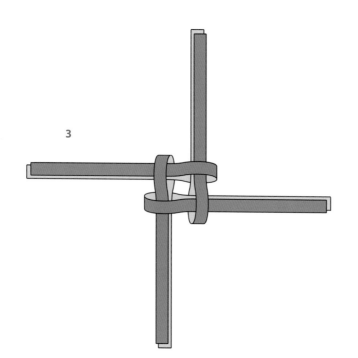

4

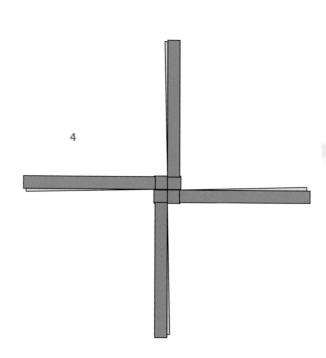

5. Cut the ends of the strips diagonally so that they are easier to weave together later on. Fold the top strip downward.

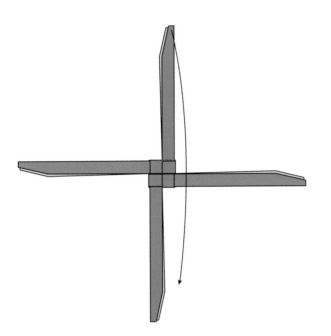

6. Continue in a clockwise direction; in other words, next fold the right-hand strip to the left.

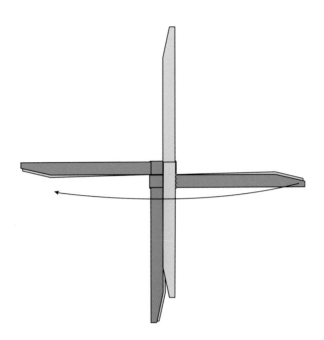

7. Fold the bottom strip upward.

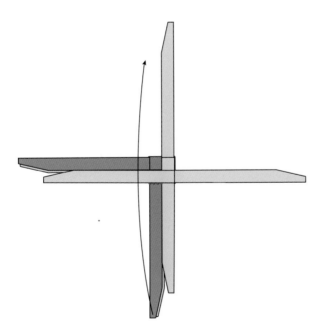

8. Fold the left-hand strip to the right and pull it through the slit that was created in step 5.

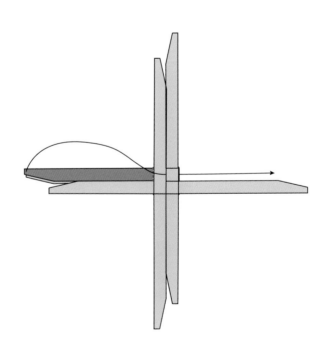

9. Fold the left top strip backward along the red line so that the strip is now parallel to the two strips on the left.

10. Now fold the same strip forward along the red line so that it is parallel to the strips coming out the bottom.

11. Fold the same strip to the right along the red line so that it lies on top of the left-hand strip coming out of the bottom.

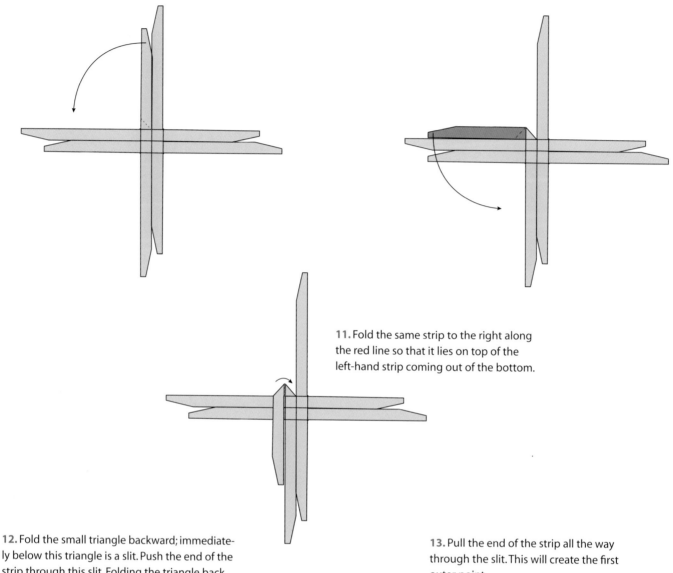

12. Fold the small triangle backward; immediately below this triangle is a slit. Push the end of the strip through this slit. Folding the triangle back gives you better access to the slit.

13. Pull the end of the strip all the way through the slit. This will create the first outer point.

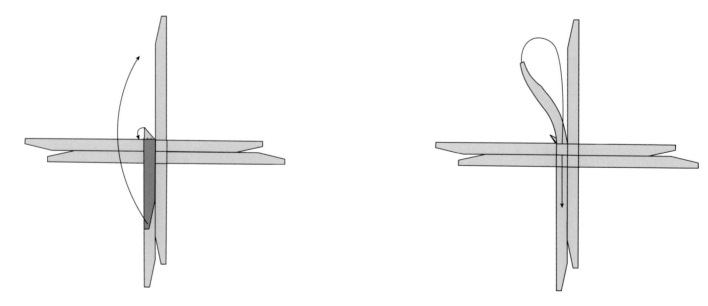

14–18. Now make the second outer point. The first folding step for the third outer point is also indicated in red here (step 18). Repeat to create the third and fourth outer points.

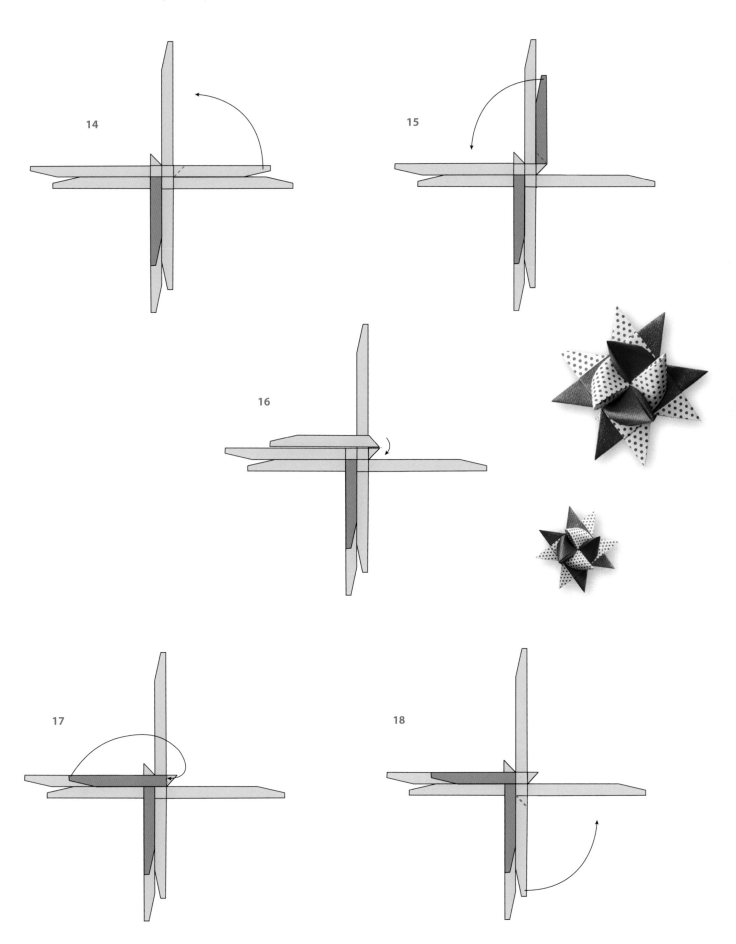

14

15

16

17

18

19. You now have four outer points. Turn the whole star over.

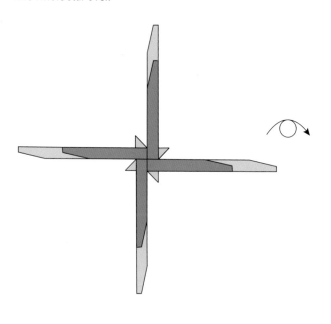

20. Make the fifth outer point exactly the same way as the first four points. Fold the top strip backward along the red line so that it is parallel to the two (stacked) strips on the left side.

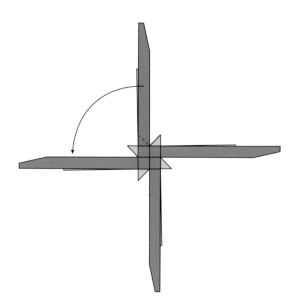

21. This time, fold the same strip forward along the red line so that it lies parallel to the strips coming out the bottom.

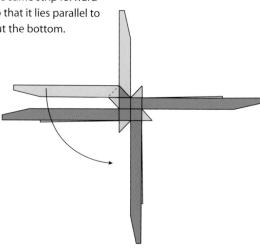

22. Fold the same strip to the right along the red line.

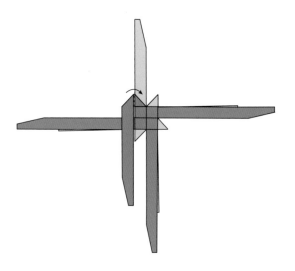

23. Fold the small triangle back; once again, there is a slit immediately below the triangle for the strip to go through.

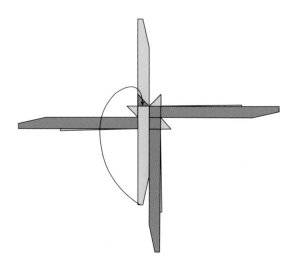

24. Pull the end of the strip through the slit. The fifth outer point is now finished. The first fold for the sixth outer point is shown here. Repeat to create the remaining outer points.

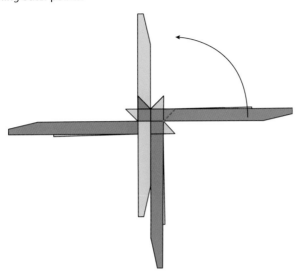

25. All eight of the outer points are now finished. Four of the outer points are covered by the strips lying on top of them. (For a Flat Fröbel Star, you would simply cut off the ends of all eight strips at this point; see page 86.)

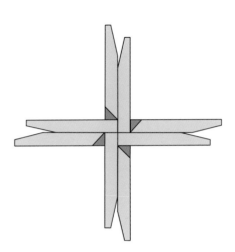

26. To make the first three-dimensional inner points, fold the top right strip downward. This reveals one of the slits.

27. Work counter-clockwise. Pull the top left strip through the slit that was just revealed.

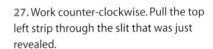

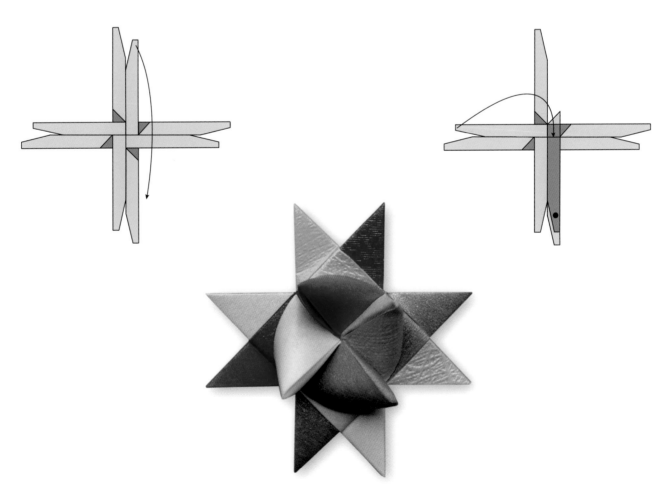

Fröbel Stars | 75

28. Slide in the strip shown in step 26 diagonally to the left so that you can see the opening (of the outer point) and the end of the strip as it emerges from the point. The insertion slit and the exit are marked by two red lines here.

Note: Sometimes it is hard to push the end of the strip through because it gets caught on a fold inside the point. You can fix this by sliding a nail file or similar flat object into the point until you can see the tip of the file. Now when you push the strip through, the nail file will keep the fold flat and let the strip slide through smoothly.

29. Pull the end of the strip tight to create a nice shape for the first inner point.

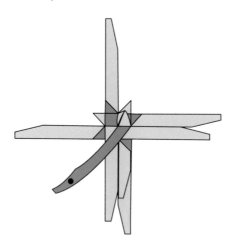

30. Repeat for the second inner point, then create the third and fourth inner points (not shown).

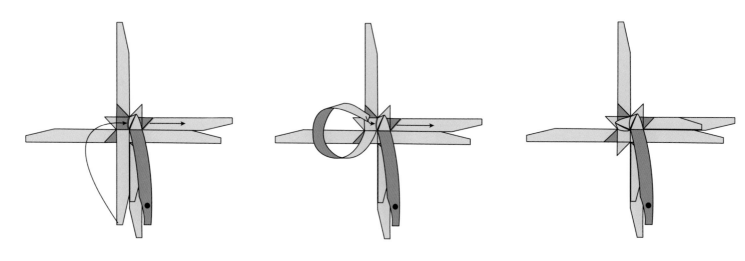

31. Now all four inner points are finished. The ends of the strips are still pointing outward, layered on top of each other in pairs. Turn the star over and make four more inner points on the other side. Now the ends of the strips are side by side in pairs.

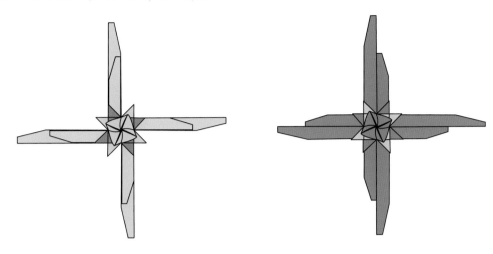

32. Trim the ends of the strips along the red lines shown here.

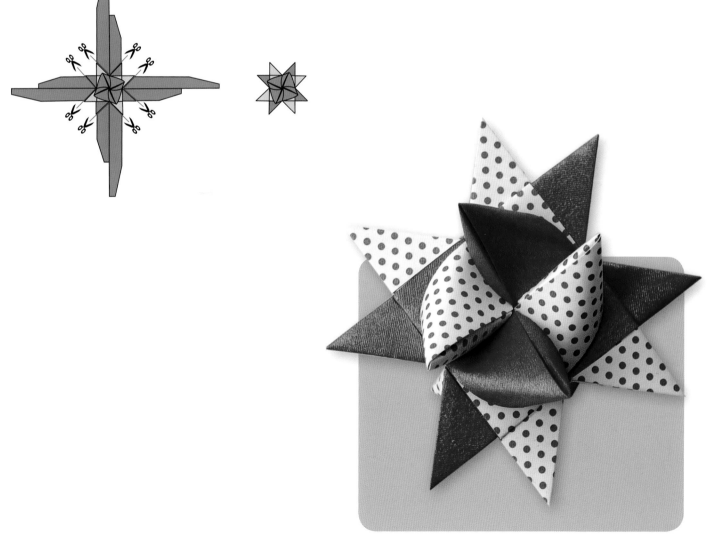

Red & White Star Decoration

◇◇

●●●

Finished Diameter

Approx. 2³/₄" (7 cm)

Materials

- 2 red paper strips and 2 red-and-white polka dot paper strips or 4 red paper strips, ²/₃" x 15³/₄" (1.5 x 40 cm)
- 2 white or dark red beads, 5 mm diameter
- Dark red bead or ²/₃" (1.5 cm) long white oval bead, 8 mm diameter
- Stiff annealed wire, 1 mm diameter and 12" (30 cm) long
- Beading glue

1. Weave together the paper strips as shown, alternating between red and polka dot strips. Make the Fröbel Star as described on the previous pages, with three-dimensional points on both sides.

2. Once the ends have been trimmed, stick the wire into the star as shown in the photo, between the points. Next, thread the beads onto the wire and attach them with a little glue if they slide down. To do so, simply slide the three beads up, apply a little glue to the wire, and then slide the beads back down over the glue.

Gold Star Decorations

◇◇◇◇◇◇◇◇◇◇◇◇◇◇◇◇◇◇◇◇◇◇◇◇◇◇◇◇◇◇◇◇◇◇◇◇◇◇

●●●
Finished Diameters
Approx. 3" (7.5 cm) and 5" (13 cm)

Materials
- 4 gold paper strips, ⅔" x 20" (1.5 x 50 cm) for the larger star, or ⅓" x 15¾" (1 x 40 cm) for the smaller star
- Stiff annealed wire, 1 mm diameter and 12" (30 cm) long
- Small piece of cardboard (for the template)
- Adhesive tape

1. Use the outline below to create a template for the spikes on the small and large stars. Photocopy the outline or trace it on transparent paper and glue it to a piece of cardboard, then cut out the template.

2. Make the Fröbel Star as described on pages 70–77, with three-dimensional points on both sides. Stick a piece of adhesive tape to each pair of strips coming out of the points so that the strips stay together while you are cutting them.

3. Turn the star and slide the template (hot pink) into one of the pairs of points with the paper strips coming out of them.

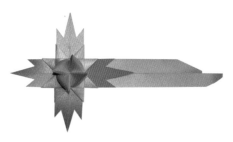

4. Cut out the spikes with a pair of scissors, following the template. Once you have cut out all of the spikes, stick the wire into the star as shown, in between the spikes.

STAR WITH LONG POINTS

●●●

Finished Diameter
Approx. 5$\frac{1}{2}$" (14 cm)

Materials
- 2 matte silver paper strips and 2 blue strips with a silver vine pattern, $\frac{3}{4}$" x 20" (2 x 50 cm)

1. Make a Fröbel Star, alternating the silver and blue strips (page 78).

2. Make the Fröbel Star with three-dimensional points on both sides (see pages 70–77). Trim all eight of the ends to 1$\frac{3}{4}$" (4.5 cm). Cut the ends of the paper strips diagonally toward the star to make the long points.

Star Ring

Finished Diameter
Ring approx. 7" (18 cm)
Star approx. 3" (7.5 cm)

Materials
• 8 sets of 4 red/gold paper strips, 1/3" x 10" (1 x 25 cm)
• All-purpose glue
• 8 paper clips or other clips to hold the stars in place for gluing

1. For each star, fold the four paper strips so that the gold side is on top. Then weave the four strips together to make a gold cross shape and pull them tight (see illustrations for the Fröbel Star on page 70, steps 1 through 4).

2. Make the Fröbel Star with three-dimensional points on both sides. Once the star is finished, trim the eight strips to 3/4" (2.2 cm) each. Cut off each strip diagonally from the end of the star to make eight even points. Make seven more stars.

3. To make a ring out of the stars, they must be arranged exactly as shown in the photo. Turn the stars so that either the gold or the red points are facing up. When arranging them, note that the distances between the points are not equal; instead, the distances between the points coming out of the star in pairs should be smaller. One of these pairs should point toward the center of the ring. The tips of the red points should overlap slightly. Ideally, clip all eight stars together. Remove one clip and glue the two stars together. Then remove the next clip and continue until all stars are glued together.

Star Mobile

●●●
Finished Diameter
Approx. 5$\frac{1}{2}$" (14 cm) for each star

Materials
- 6 Fröbel Stars made from paper strips $\frac{1}{2}$" x 15" (1.25 x 38 cm)
- Mobile wire arms, 6" (15 cm), 8" (20 cm) and 10" (25 cm) long
- Nylon thread, 0.25 mm thick
- Punching needle
- Small hooks
- One large suspension hook

1. Tie a large suspension hook to the end of a 15$\frac{3}{4}$" (40 cm) long thread, then tie the thread to the middle of the 10" (25 cm) long wire arm, about 4" (10 cm) down. Do not trim the remaining thread—you will be hanging a star from it.

2. Tie a very small hook to one end of a 12" (30 cm) long thread. About 2$\frac{3}{4}$" (7 cm) down, tie the thread to the middle of the 8" (20 cm) long wire arm. You will tie the top star to the end of this thread later.

3. Tie a thread with a very small hook to the middle of the third wire arm, about 4" (10 cm) down.

4. Hang up the long wire arm. Attach one of the smaller wire arms to each end, using the small hooks.

5. Prepare the threads for hanging the stars. Cut four threads about 12" (30 cm) long and tie a small hook to the end of each (these hooks will later be attached to the ends of the wire arm). Punch holes in the stars, pulling the other end of the thread through the hole and tying it off. Be sure that the distance between the hook and the star is different for each star.

6. Hang the four stars that are attached to the threads to the ends of the wire arms, using the small hooks. Tie the two remaining stars to the two threads hanging from the middle of the long- and medium-sized wire arms.

COMET

Finished Size
Approx. 6½" (17 cm) with tail

Materials
- 4 strips of red paper with white snowflakes, ¾" x 20" (2 x 50 cm)
- All-purpose glue

1. Make the three-dimensional star as described on pages 70–77 and cut off seven of the strip ends, leaving the longest strip (the ends are different lengths).

2. Take the longest two strips that you have already cut off and stick them into the same point with the remaining strip.

3. Fan out the three strips and glue them together. Then cut the ends of the three strips diagonally, at the same angle.

MULTICOLORED FRÖBEL STAR

●●●

Finished Diameter
Approx. 1¹/₂" (4 cm)

Materials
• 4 strips of paper: 1 white, 1 silver, 1 gold, and 1 red, ¹/₃" x 10" (1 x 25 cm)

1. Weave together the four paper strips in a cross shape, in the order shown.

2. Make the Fröbel Star with three-dimensional points on both sides (pages 70–77).

FLAT FRÖBEL STAR

Finished Diameter

Approx. 2⅓" (6 cm)

Materials

• 4 strips of paper, 2 in each color, e.g. in light blue and white, ½" x 12" (1.5 x 30 cm)

1. Flat Fröbel Stars can be used as gift tags and Christmas tree ornaments as well as for decorating cards. Make the Fröbel Star as described on pages 70–77, up to step 25. Then trim the ends of the strips to match the width of the strips—here, ½" (1.5 cm).

2. Fold one of these square strip ends (silver-gray in the photo) to the left.

3. Fold this square diagonally to the right.

4. Fold the resulting triangle to the right.

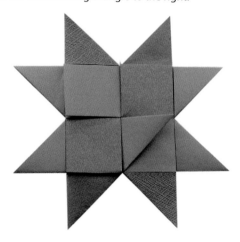

5. Repeat with the remaining three squares.

POP-UP STAR NOTE CARD AND GIFT TAG

●●●

Finished Diameter
Star approx. 2¹⁄₃" (6 cm)

Materials
- 4 strips of white paper with a green pattern, ¹⁄₂" x 15³⁄₄" (1.5 x 40 cm), for each star
- Light green folded note cards, 8" x 4" (20 x 10 cm) and 8" x 6" (20 x 15 cm), before folding

- Red cardboard squares, 3" x 3" (8 x 8 cm)
- Red cardboard circle, 3" (7.5 cm) diameter
- Light green cardboard circle, 3³⁄₄" (9.5 cm) diameter
- Red cord, 2–3 mm thick, 12" (30 cm) long
- Red bead, 5–6 mm diameter
- Hole punch
- All-purpose glue

1. Make each star according to the instructions on pages 70–77, up to step 31. Only make one side of the star three-dimensional, skipping the three-dimensional inner points on the other side. That gives the star a flat side so it can be glued onto a card or other object.

2. Cut the four strips that are coming out of the points flush with the points. Turn the star over. Either cut off the four remaining strips flush with the points or leave ¹⁄₂" (1.5 cm) of each (corresponding to the width of the strip) and glue the four square strip ends to the back of the star. Glue a red bead to the center of the star.

3. For the two light green cards, fold in half to make them 4" x 4" (10 x 10 cm) and 6" x 4" (15 x 10 cm). Glue a red cardboard square to the front of each card, rounding the edges if desired. Finally, glue on the Fröbel Star.

   To make the circle tag, glue the red circle onto the light green circle, and glue the star onto the red circle.

4. Punch a hole in the top left corner of each gift tag and pull the cord through.

Frobel Stars | 89

About the Author

Armin Täubner lives with his family in the Swabian Alps in Germany and has worked successfully as a freelance author for more than 25 years.

He is primarily a teacher of English, biology, and visual arts. Täubner became interested in making books thanks to his wife, author Inge Walz. Without a doubt, a win for the creative world! Almost every medium sparks Armin Täubner's imagination, and he can master almost any technique within a short amount of time. However, his favorite material will always be paper.

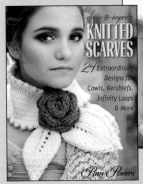